PASTORELLA
A Play about Unfamous Actors

by

Stuart Eugene Bousel

EXIT
PRESS
SAN FRANCISCO

Pastorella
by Stuart Eugene Bousel
Copyright © 2013 by Stuart Eugene Bousel
All rights reserved

Published by EXIT PRESS

First Production of *Pastorella* was by No Nude Men Productions,
October 9, 2014, at EXIT Stage Left, The EXIT Theatre, in San
Francisco, California. Directed by Stuart Bousel.

Cover design by Cody Rishell
Book design by Richard Livingston and C White

For performance inquiries, contact Stuart Eugene Bousel at
bouselstuart@gmail.com

For additional information about the EXIT PRESS,
go to www.exitpress.org

Paperback ISBN: 978-1-941704-17-2

EXIT PRESS
156 Eddy Street
San Francisco, CA 94102-2708
mail@theexit.org

First Edition: April 2018

Dedicated to
Christina, Amanda, Richard:

What we do here is real.

FOREWORD

by Ariel Craft

Stuart Bousel's *Pastorella* is a love letter, equal parts tender and fraught, to indie theatre.

For those who've cut teeth, chiseled artistic identities, and made homes in the indie theatre: the play might make us chuckle and cringe with recognition, as it needles the insecurities that we strive to stave off.

What does success look like?

When will I stop pursuing an artistic life and start living an artistic life?

Am I enough? Is what I'm doing enough? Is this place enough?

And Bousel doesn't impose arbitrary conclusions or an unearned sense of peace upon us or the play's characters: he lets these questions float and waft—as they do, truly, through the daily experiences of such artists—for us to contend with, individually and personally.

What he does leave us with is a call to action:

Don't ever wait for someone else to grant you permission to create something.

Think of how many stories, how many voices have been lost in the limbo of awaiting validation.

Make something now—something that matters to you—where you are now.

The most fundamental, essential building block of theatre is a group of people, committed to coming together—bringing what they have to contribute, without reservation—in the creation of a shared vision.

Art and expression belong everywhere that people can be found.

And we should look for it, everywhere.

And value it, everywhere.

AUTHOR'S NOTE

I wrote the first draft of this play—which was originally three acts!—in about a week. It's about as close to a stream-of-conscious play as I have ever written and it took three revisions (and the cutting of one character) to get it to a point where it was as sharp and funny as I wanted it to be. "Sharp" being the key word because of all my comedies this is arguably the most biting and satirical. Basically, all of my hate for the small theater community (and there's a lot that I've acquired over 20 years of working in it) was poured into this show, with lampoons of some of my favorite, and least favorite, collaborators and partners, selected from shows and companies past and Frankensteined into the backstage comedy archetypes of the Stage Mother, the New Kid, the Old Salt, the Bit Player, The Ingenue, The Token Person of Color, and so forth. Of course, because I love the theater (and the small theater world in particular) there is also a great deal of pride and love and bittersweet humor poured into the play, and I love all of the characters in this show—even sour, dour Josh and his fierce determination to be a "real" actor, no matter what it might cost him. The closing scene, where Gwen and Warren stand in the empty dressing room, mourning the end of one show and planning the next, epitomizes for me the bittersweet hopefulness of a life in the Arts, where you are between projects more often than you are in them, and where Art itself tends to matter much less than mundane concerns like fame and fortune. And yet for some reason, against all odds, you keep coming back to do it again and again.

PASTORELLA

A play about unfamous actors

FIRST STAGED READING OF PASTORELLA:

No Nude Men Productions, March 30, 2013, part of the "Behind the Curtain" series at The EXIT Theatre, in San Francisco, California.

Directed by Anthony Miller.

MARCH 2013 CAST:

John Caldon	**WARREN ALVING**
Annika Bergman	**GWEN HOWARD**
Peter Townley	**JOSH BAKER**
Charles Lewis III	**CLIFF SAMUEL**
Andrew Chung	**ROY WANG**
Carole Swann	**BETTINA SNELL**
Kate Jones	**ELECTRA SNELL**
Anthony Pinggera	**TOBY KENT**
Allene Hebert	**ANYA MONROE**
Jeremy Cole	**LANCE MONROE**

FIRST PRODUCTION:

*No Nude Men Productions, October 9, 10, 11, 16, 17, 18, 23, 24, 25, 2014, at the EXIT Stage Left, The EXIT Theatre, in San Francisco, California.

Stuart Bousel	Director
Linda Huang	Stage Manager
Cody Rishell	Art
William Campbell	Lighting Design

OCTOBER 2014 CAST:

Larissa Archer .... **ANYA MONROE**

Nathan Brown .... **JOSH BAKER**

Katrina Bushnell .... **GWEN HOWARD**

Ben Calabrese .... **TOBY KENT**

Andrew Chung .... **ROY WANG**

Valerie Fachman .... **BETTINA SNELL**

Justin Gillman .... **WARREN ALVING**

Charles Lewis III .... **CLIFF SAMUEL**

Brandice Thompson.... **ELECTRA SNELL**

*The premiere production of *Pastorella* was a 2015, Theatre Bay Area Award Finalist for Outstanding World Premier of A Play.

CAST OF CHARACTERS

WARREN ALVING: 29, charismatic, intense, mildly alcoholic, plays Valentine in the play, is Josh's boyfriend

GWEN HOWARD: 23, attractive, friendly, shy, plays Chloe in the play, is one year out of college

JOSH BAKER: 26, handsome, extroverted, temperamental, plays Septimus in the play, is Warren's lover

CLIFF SAMUEL: 35, African-American, dignified, articulate, patient, plays Noakes in the play, is also the stage manager and has been with the company longer than anyone but the owners

BETTINA SNELL: 44, English, stately, acerbic, powerful, plays Lady Croom in the play, is Electra's mother

ELECTRA SNELL: 17, American, pretty, smart, universally angry, plays Thomasina in the play, is Bettina's daughter

ROY WANG: 32, Asian American, hyper-masculine, confident, provocative, plays Jellaby in the play

TOBY KENT: 20, exuberant, positive, innocent, plays Gus in the play, which is the first one he's ever been in

ANYA MONROE: 38, Latin American, composed, efficient, intelligent, plays Hannah in the play, co-runs the company with her husband, Lance Monroe

SCENE ONE: DRESS

The dressing room of a reasonably well-funded, small theater company. Perhaps a bit larger than typical, but equitably as crowded, doubling as storage and workspace. Tables, chairs, neatly stacked boxes of things. GWEN is applying eye-liner to WARREN, who sits in a chair. On the other side of the room sits ELECTRA, talking on her phone. GWEN and WARREN are in their twenties, though he is older. They wear contemporary clothes that are costumes. ELECTRA is in a regency period dress. She is a teenager.

GWEN: I want theater to have the immediacy of music.

ELECTRA: No, Dina, I get it, it's a big deal, and of course I really want to do it, I really really do, but I'm in this show, right, and it's like opening that night, right, and I'm like not able to miss that so—can we reschedule the shoot, because I'd really love that, right?

GWEN: I want that sense you get when you go to a concert—like a really good concert—and you feel that connection with the singer and the crowd.

ELECTRA: See, like, I don't have an understudy, right? None of us have understudies. It's like the theater, Dina, not Broadway.

GWEN: That connection that makes you feel like the singer is singing only for you and yet, at the same time, you know that everyone else in the audience is feeling what you're feeling too and it becomes all about community and just being alive together.

ELECTRA: It's like a lead role, right, Dina, they can't just do it without me, right?

GWEN: That's how theater should work too. Every time I see a show I should feel like I'm part of the community of the alive.

ELECTRA: Look, Dina, I love you, right, but I sent you a schedule three months ago, right, and I don't understand why you're scheduling me for shit I can't do, right?

GWEN: Not that every concert is utterly amazing, of course, but I do think there is something about music that is just so direct, so immediate, and even when it's kind of terrible, it's still really vital.

ELECTRA: This is such bullshit, right? How much money do I make for you, right? No, please, I want, like, an actual figure, right.

GWEN: When I am onstage I want to feel very powerful and very alive. I want to believe in what I am doing. And I want the audience to feel that too.

ELECTRA: What? What did you just say? No really, bitch, repeat thyself.

GWEN: Close your eyes. (*she blows on his face*) Open. Perfect.

ELECTRA: Well fuck you too, Dina, and fuck your fucking agency! Stay obscure, bitch, I don't give a fuck anymore! (*ELECTRA throws her phone across the room. A long moment, and then she screams:*) MOM!

    ELECTRA exits.

GWEN: What do you suppose is going to happen with that?

WARREN: I don't know. I was paying attention to you because I hate her. Mirror?

GWEN: Hold on. (*she grabs a hand mirror from a nearby table*) There you go.

WARREN: (*he looks at himself*) Well done. I don't look like a pharaoh or a whore.

GWEN: I told you I was good.

WARREN: Good? This is like a small theater miracle. Thank you.

GWEN: How come you can't do your own? Didn't they teach you in school?

WARREN: I was an English major.

GWEN: I thought you were a Theater major.

WARREN: Josh was the Theater major. He went to Julliard.

GWEN: Oh, that's right. He told me that at the first read through. Several times.

WARREN: That's my boy!

GWEN: I think he said it like five times.

WARREN: That's because you were supposed to say, "Wow, how impressive, what the fuck are you doing here?" You see, Josh suffers best for his art when he knows someone has read and understood his bio. Anyway, it doesn't matter, because you like me best.

GWEN: I like you both.

WARREN: But you like me best. Admit it.

GWEN: Fine. I do.

WARREN: Hurray! The young man leaps from his seat with joy. Though he suspects it's only because he needs the young woman to do his make-up, and she suffers best for her art when she feels needed by someone.

GWEN: Probably true. If there's one thing I have learned from television it's that skill validation only really means something if it comes from bitchy homosexuals.

WARREN: I am never bitchy. I am snarky and there is a difference. Josh is bitchy.

GWEN: Josh is bitchy.

WARREN: Josh is mean.

GWEN: Well, I wouldn't say that.

WARREN: I would. Look, it's okay to hate Josh. We all kind of hate Josh. I mean, I love him, desperately, but I also kind of hate him. So you can totally hate him. I encourage you to hate him. I want you to hate him.

GWEN: I don't hate anybody.

WARREN: Liar.

GWEN: I don't.

WARREN: Saying you don't hate somebody is like saying you don't love somebody. Sometimes I hate Josh more than I hate anyone in the world. More than I hate Electra. More than I hate Bettina, and I really fucking hate her. More than I hate all those obnoxious TV fags you so desperately want validation from. Validation you'll never get and shouldn't want because they're all terrible. Every last one of them. Though secretly, I'm worse than all of them. You just don't know it yet.

GWEN: See, you are a bitchy homosexual.

WARREN: No, that was snark. I suffer best for my art when I convince you I hate everyone in the world but you.

> *ROY ducks his head in. He is also in period clothes, dressed as a butler. He is Asian-American, in his early thirties.*

ROY: Hey niggas, anyone seen Lance? Cuntasina and Ladycunt are having a throw down on stage and it looks like there's gonna be blood.

GWEN: Did you just call us… that word?

ROY: Yup.

WARREN: It just never gets old for you, does it? Lance is probably in the booth.

ROY: Nope. Hence the looking and the asking.

WARREN: Have you asked Anya?

ROY: She doesn't know where he is. She's been sitting in the house finishing Bettina's dress since I got here.

GWEN: Oh shit, I was supposed to help with that.

ROY: Whatevs. Bettina's not gonna notice. She's too busy putting on her one woman show, "Bitchslapping My Daughter In Public."

GWEN: That sounds more like a two woman show.

ROY: Nah, in the full production, Electra doesn't have any lines. She just stands there and takes it up the ass silently, so you can just *Cloud 9* that shit with a dummy.

WARREN: God, Roy, stop stealing pages from my production journal!

ROY: Sorry Boo, but a man has to wipe his ass with something. Listen, I gotta find Lance, but you should probably get out there. Shit is going down.

WARREN: We're not getting involved. I've made that decision for Gwen. Please just call us when it's time to do some acting.

ROY: Home Slice, I ain't the stage manager.

WARREN: Well if you see that cocksucker in your rambles just let him know we're in here, would you, Woo?

ROY: Anyone ever tell you that eyeliner makes you look gay? 'Cause it do.

ROY exits.

GWEN: Do you think we should go out there?

WARREN: I'm not in Scene One. Are you in Scene One?

GWEN: No, I mean, Bettina and—

WARREN: Let Lance handle it. Trust me. This sort of shit happens all the time.

GWEN: Really?

WARREN: The young man shrugs and smiles sheepishly, embarrassed by the lack of professionalism in his company.

GWEN: I just assumed this kind of thing ended after college.

WARREN: Ha-ha, no. Divas be brawling. Everywhere there's a company, divas be brawling. But hey, what a stipend, right?

GWEN: I'm not complaining.

WARREN: You shouldn't. We have really good stipends here.

GWEN: I know. I was kind of shocked. Especially for community theater.

WARREN: Honey, we've had this talk. I know you're Fresh Off The College, but this is indie theater. If this was community theater, there wouldn't be any stipends, and we'd have a make-up person.

GWEN takes the mirror from WARREN and sets it on the table. She picks up a hair brush and brushes her hair while he watches.

GWEN: I love doing make-up. It's how I earned all my crew hours at the U.

WARREN: I've never been good with it. My senior year, on the opening night of *Cabaret*, I tried to do it myself. I cried all through Act One because I had jabbed my eye ten times before curtain.

GWEN: It takes practice. Eyes are the hardest part to do.

WARREN: I was just trying to put on lipstick.

GWEN: Nobody is that clumsy.

WARREN: I'm close. I'm fairly certain the only reason I didn't get Septimus is because Lance knows I can't dance and he didn't want the show ending with me knocking over the set. Plus Josh auditioned, even though he told me he wasn't going to.

GWEN: Who did you play in *Cabaret*?

WARREN: Ernst.

GWEN: Really?

WARREN: No, I'm lying because it's such a glamorous role. Yeah, I played Ernst. That's like the Warren Alving role to a tee.

GWEN: I played Fraulien Kost in college. If we had been in the same production, we would have had a duet together.

WARREN: If I directed that show, I'd probably have a drag queen play her.

GWEN: And take the quintessential Gwen Howard role away from me? Thanks.

WARREN: Whatever, I'd cast you as Sally Bowles.

GWEN: Really?

WARREN: Duh. And then I could be your Cliff. Of course, there's that fucking Telephone Dance so I'd never get it. Josh would. And then I'd have to watch you two fall in love and abort your baby. Never mind, bad plan. Let's just do 'Night Mother instead.

GWEN: It really bothers you that Josh beat you out for Septimus, doesn't it?

WARREN: He didn't beat me, he just knows how to waltz. And he's very good looking. (*beat*) Valentine's a really good role so I am not complaining, I just I think I would have been fucking awesome as Septimus—even opposite Electra. But the character doesn't matter. It's *Arcadia*. That's what matters. Who doesn't want to be in *Arcadia*, right?

GWEN: I never did. I mean, Hanna's the only really good female role and she's old.

WARREN: She's barely middle-aged.

GWEN: She's like forty.

WARREN: I'm turning thirty on opening night.

GWEN: (*excited*) You are?

WARREN: Extinguish the birthday candles that just lit in your mind.

GWEN: What's wrong with turning thirty?

WARREN: Nothing. If you're happy. Back to Stoppard. Chloe's not a bad part.

GWEN: No, she's fun. I mean, it's a way better role than Fraulien Kost. But I didn't show up hoping to get her or anything. I hadn't even read the play until I was cast. I just audition for everything. And Lance was the only person who cast me this season. Even though I auditioned for twenty-eight shows. That was eye-opening. Would I have preferred to play Juliet over at the Rep? Sure. But I'm happy to be here.

WARREN: They missed out.

GWEN: There was a lot of competition. And I'm not a great auditioner.

WARREN: Is anyone? I mean, I've watched a lot of auditions. It has a lot less to do with how good you are than most actors want to admit.

GWEN: Well who wants to admit that it's all about who we know or the way we look?

WARREN: Who says it's about that? I would posture that most good directors ignore the monologues or whatever and just focus on the person and try to see if they can see something exceptional or interesting.

There's a quality, star quality, I guess, that you try to hone in on. And if an actor doesn't have the right quality then you probably aren't going to cast them, no matter how good the skills on display. Without the right quality, the rest is just a sack of tricks. And like, a dog can learn tricks, you know?

JOSH enters, also in period wear. He is strikingly good looking, in his mid-twenties.

JOSH: Please tell me we're back to not-not-smoking this week.

WARREN: The young man turns and smiles at the love of his life. Actually, I'm doing a fantastic job of not-smoking this week. So… sorry, babe.

JOSH: We're in dress rehearsals. You always smoke in dress rehearsal. I rely on this.

WARREN: Only when I'm directing. When I act I'm on vacation, remember?

JOSH: You smoked all the way through *Angels*.

WARREN: Only because I was playing Louis. (*to GWEN*) I had wanted to play Joe.

GWEN: Who played Joe?

JOSH: I played Joe.

GWEN: Well, Louis is the better part anyway.

JOSH/WARREN: No he isn't.

JOSH: Louis has more lines but he's neurotic and nebbishy and you know you're just playing Tony Kushner.

WARREN: Whereas Joe is clearly Tony Kushner's guilty little sex fantasy.

JOSH: Which means Joe is just intrinsically sexier.

WARREN: Yeah, getting to play Joe is like public declaration that you're sexy.

JOSH: It's like having Tony Kushner publicly declare that you are sexy.

GWEN: I've wanted to play Harper since high school.

JOSH: Obviously. (*to WARREN*) So neither of us has cigarettes?

WARREN: For the last nine days I have been doing a really good job quitting smoking by the time I'm thirty and you should be supportive of that. Perhaps by not taking up smoking just because it's tech week, only so you can abandon it once we open, but just in time for me to have started smoking again.

JOSH: How did you make this about you?

WARREN: The young man looks askance at the love of his life.

JOSH: Stop doing that. It's so twee.

WARREN: The young man shrugs and smiles sheepishly.

JOSH: Toby smokes, doesn't he?

WARREN: He sure does.

JOSH: TOBY!

He exits.

WARREN: Well, Josh is agitated. That can't be good.

GWEN: I don't think he likes me very much.

WARREN: It's not personal. He takes a long time to win over.

GWEN: How did you win him over?

WARREN: We were in *Hamlet* together. The first time Lance cast either of us, actually. He was Hamlet. Duh. I was Laertes. There was a lot of fight choreography. We were both making a play for the fight choreographer. Who turned out to be straight. We made the best of the situation, went to a bar to be humiliated together, got drunk, fucked in my car, and realized we liked each other.

GWEN: A theater romance.

WARREN: A classic theater romance. For three months we spoke almost entirely in quotations from the *Complete Works*.

GWEN: It's always lovely in the beginning isn't it?

WARREN: Yes. Absolutely. We had a great honeymoon period. We did like three shows in a row together, and then Lance asked me to start directing here and Josh and I used to stay up all night, talking about my concept for shows and who he'd play and…

A long moment.

GWEN: We're way over due for call. We should go out there.

WARREN: I don't want to. There's something in the air and I always feel the safest in here. Besides, everything major happens backstage, and if it's important, it'll come to us.

ROY and CLIFF enter, both in full period wear.
CLIFF carries a clipboard and wears a headset.
He is African-American, in his mid-thirties.

CLIFF: We are on dinner break. Feel free to be back in half an hour.

WARREN: (*to GWEN*) See?

GWEN: But we haven't even done Act One!

CLIFF: And considering Act One is ninety minutes long, I'd say we're gonna be here till midnight. Which means I'm gonna be here till three. Yaaaayyyyy.

ROY: Sucks to be you, Negro.

CLIFF: What have I said about you calling me that?

ROY: I don't know. I don't listen to other people when they talk. Homo, Girlfriend—you want to hit the pizza trough?

GWEN: I don't eat gluten.

WARREN: I only eat cupcakes and beer.

ROY: Want me to pick you up a six-pack on the way back?

WARREN: Cliff?

CLIFF: I need you both sober.

BETTINA, half in costume, half out, storms in. She is almost fifty, the oldest person in the building, and has a British accent. She actually is British, but the accent is still fake.

BETTINA: Though I have spent the last twenty minutes being verbally assaulted by my own daughter while nobody bothered to intervene—I have prevailed. Thanks to me, our opening night remains on schedule and the show can still be a success. Remember this when the *BroadwayWorld* nominations come out.

CLIFF: (*to ROY, opening his wallet*) Make it a case, Roy.

WARREN: (*throwing in some money*) Make it two. And no cider.

ROY: Fuck you, homie, you know I don't drink that shit.

WARREN: Crispin is a cider, Roy.

ROY: No, it's a Shakespeare reference and therefore, it's cool. (*passing BETTINA*) You want a hot slice, girl? I'm heading to the food wagon.

BETTINA: I do not speak *The Wire*.

ROY: Just asking. See y'all in an hour.

CLIFF: Half an hour.

ROY: What's that? Hour and a half. Got it.

ROY exits.

BETTINA: Where is he going? He's in the first scene. Practically the first page.

CLIFF: We're on dinner break. You may not have heard over the shouting.

BETTINA: When did we go on dinner break?

CLIFF: About ten minutes ago.

BETTINA: Why on earth would you send everyone on dinner break now?

CLIFF: Because we couldn't start the play with you and Electra screaming at one another on the stage.

BETTINA: At least I was doing something! (*to WARREN*) She was going to quit.

CLIFF: She wasn't going to quit.

BETTINA: She wanted us to postpone opening. It's as good as quitting.

GWEN: Why did she want to—?

BETTINA: Some stupid gum advert that awful agent of hers booked without bothering to ask first. As if the theater stops because the television needs to cross the road.

WARREN: Again? The same thing happened when we were doing *The Secret Garden*—

CLIFF: I wasn't going to say it.

WARREN: Why does she keep agreeing to be in these shows when she wants to be in commercials and she's clearly getting enough work to need to plan for that?

BETTINA: Until she is eighteen, Mr. Alving, my daughter doesn't work unless I agree that she works. And while I appreciate the money and the exposure and the regrettable but necessary camera training resulting from the few acceptable adverts I have allowed her to take, the fact is, I have not instructed Electra in the brilliance of Shakespeare and Stanislavsky so that she can be some mincing, vapid, over-lit cud-chewing poppet.

WARREN: Did you just use the word poppet?

BETTINA: You know what it means, Mr. Alving. You're a mediocre actor but we both know you're very well-read.

CLIFF: What the hell is a poppet?

WARREN: Seriously dude? *The Crucible*?

CLIFF: The last time I checked there was only one Black role in that show and it wasn't for a guy, dude.

BETTINA: There are no Black roles in *Arcadia*, Mr. Samuel and yet here you are.

CLIFF: Noakes is barely a character.

BETTINA: And considering your attempts at a British accent are barely acceptable, I would say it's your principal role as stage manager that landed you any role in the show at all.

CLIFF: You know I didn't audition. Lance asked me to play this role because he felt bad asking an actor to put in a full rehearsal period for such a minuscule part. Since I was already going to be here, it just made the most sense.

BETTINA: Well congratulations. Should we ever do *The Crucible*, I shall encourage him to envision you doing a high-pitched Harry Belafonte in turban and petticoats.

CLIFF: If you ever hate on Belafonte again I will make sure you are poisoned on closing night.

BETTINA: Good luck with that, Mr. Samuel. I have played Cleopatra five times. Nothing can kill me.

WARREN: Honestly, Lance should have just cut the role entirely. It's not like the play isn't long enough to stand some trimming.

BETTINA: We do not cut Mr. Stoppard, Mr. Alving. Just as we do not cut Mr. Shakespeare.

WARREN: I cut Mr. Shakespeare all the time.

BETTINA: What you do isn't actually Shakespeare, Mr. Alving. It's Mr. Alving trying to be edgy with Shakespeare because he can not acquire the rights to manhandle Samuel Beckett or The Green Day.

GWEN: Is she talking about the band?

WARREN: She has no idea what she's talking about.

CLIFF: Where is Electra?

BETTINA: Sulking where I left her. When is this disaster supposed to begin?

CLIFF: I think it started around thirty years ago.

BETTINA: Mr. Samuel, I am talking about rehearsal, not your life.

CLIFF: We're back at eight-thirty. (*to WARREN*) Make sure I get some of that beer.

WARREN: No beer in the booth. You know that's a rule, Cliff.

CLIFF: I wish I could be in the booth for this show.

BETTINA: We wish you could be too.

GWEN: I'll make sure they don't drink it all, Cliff.

CLIFF: Thank you.

GWEN: Is there anything else you need help with?

CLIFF: If you want to stay late you can kick the step-ladder out from under my feet.

GWEN: Why would I do that?

BETTINA: He's threatening to hang himself.

GWEN: Oh! I thought maybe it was a lighting thing I didn't know about.

WARREN: Man, don't hang yourself in the theater. You know none of us would know how to cut you down. We'd have to ask Candace, or that kid running the box office.

CLIFF: His name is Stanley. And you're all cutting into your dinner break.

TOBY enters. He's in contemporary clothes. He bumps into CLIFF, who is exiting.

TOBY: Hey Cliff!

CLIFF: I'm on dinner break.

TOBY: Yeah. I knew that.

CLIFF: Then why are you talking to me?

CLIFF exits. TOBY turns to everyone.

TOBY: He's having a tough night.

WARREN: We know.

GWEN: Don't take it personally.

TOBY: Oh, I don't. I've seen *Slings and Arrows*. I know that stage managers have a really heavy load on their plate and they're basically doing all the dirty work so that the glue that holds a production together can actually stick. Plus he's playing a part, which I think is totally awesome but whoa, right, what a crazy thing to have to do when you're already doing something else, something really essential, and you're not really an actor to begin with. I can't imagine what he's going through, but I can tell he's gonna make it all work and then he's gonna be able to relax and we're gonna be like, "Wow man, you did it!" and it's gonna be awesome.

WARREN: Right. Where's Josh?

TOBY: He and Roy went to get pizza together.

WARREN: Cool.

TOBY: Yeah, it seemed okay. Like, I don't think they're screwing around or anything.

WARREN: Um… okay.

TOBY: Roy's a good looking guy, but I don't get the cheating vibe off of Josh, and I definitely get the vaguely homophobic vibe off of Roy. Like, not in a beat up gay guys way, but in a, I'm-gonna-watch-what-I-drink-around-you sort of way. Also, even though I know there's a lot of messing around in the theater, I feel like this cast is sort of above that, you know? Partly because you two are both queer and Electra's jailbait even for me—oh hey Mrs. Snell—but also 'cause there's a lot of real respect here for one another, you know, like there was in *Fellowship*. Those guys are just getting pizza together like the way Sean Bean and Viggo Mortensen would go fishing together between takes. You don't have anything to worry about.

WARREN: Thanks for… that.

TOBY: Everything okay with Electra?

BETTINA: She'll be fine. And we'll be opening as scheduled.

WARREN: First we need to get through this rehearsal.

BETTINA: Over-dramatics are entirely unnecessary. You know first dress is never easy.

GWEN: She's right.

BETTINA: No one asked you for an endorsement, Miss Howard.

GWEN: Sorry?

BETTINA: Less art and less matter, please.

GWEN: Did you just tell me to shut up?

WARREN: Let it go, Gwen, she's senile. (*to BETTINA*) Listen, the usual bullshit with your devilspawn aside, you don't think there's like a weird, crazy, shit is gonna get real vibe in the air?

TOBY: Personally, I think it's awesome. I mean, yeah, it kind of sucks that all this crap is going down and there is all this tension, but you always hear about how in movies and plays and stuff there's like all this stuff that happens and like people get all angry and stuff breaks and doesn't get done and then it all comes together and out of nowhere you have like, this miracle and stuff just works and bam you're done and everyone claps and you get an Oscar and when you talk about it during the interviews for the DVD extras it's like magic! Personally, I'm so pumped for that and I'm sure you guys are too so from the way I see it we're kind of right on schedule and this is just exactly the way I knew it was going to be.

WARREN: Yeah… I'd probably be a little more pumped if it wasn't five past eight and I knew where Lance was.

BETTINA: What do you mean?

WARREN: Lance is gone. Or never arrived.

BETTINA: He's been sitting in the booth going over cues with Candace.

WARREN: Are you sure about that?

BETTINA: If you're asking if I've actually seen him then the answer is no, but he's the director, where else would he be?

WARREN: Considering he's also the producer and he's playing Bernard—he should be back here putting on make-up. But he hasn't been. How did you not notice?

BETTINA: Am I here to notice the whereabouts of everyone in the building?

GWEN: He's the director.

BETTINA: I know the nature of Mr. Monroe's position.

WARREN: Yes, but do you know what his current position is?

TOBY: Ha! Dude, that was awesome. Gay guys are just as funny as I hoped they'd be.

WARREN: I wasn't making a joke there.

TOBY: Oh. I thought you were being dirty.

BETTINA: I'm certain wherever Mr. Monroe is, he's on the premises.

WARREN: Roy was looking for him earlier. And he wasn't here when I got here.

BETTINA: Who opened the theater?

GWEN: I helped Anya load in some of the costumes. We were the first people here.

WARREN: Lance wasn't with Anya?

BETTINA: That doesn't mean anything. Not all married couples travel in packs. I haven't seen my husband in years.

WARREN: So what you're saying is that Anya may have killed Lance?

TOBY: I don't know. They seem like a happy couple to me. Like Peter and his wife.

BETTINA: Peter who?

WARREN: Jackson. (*to TOBY*) Am I right?

TOBY: Duh. (*realizing something*) Whoa.

GWEN: You know, when I picked her up today, Anya did seem kind of… off.

BETTINA: It's the week before opening and she has had to finish two dozen regency costumes she made from the thin air—while also rehearsing to play the female lead in a play that is not exactly short-winded. Only an amateur would expect her to look anything less than exhausted.

GWEN: Or there really is something wrong at home.

TOBY: Wait—Lance is dead?

WARREN: Okay, so, that was a joke, Toby. At least when I said it. Five minutes ago.

GWEN: Maybe they're fighting or something. They've both had so much on their plates. And I've always heard it's a really bad thing to work with your partner.

WARREN: Josh and I do it all the time.

TOBY: Oh, now I get it.

GWEN: Yeah and there are definitely never any issues there.

TOBY: Wait—did Bettina kill her husband?

BETTINA: Sadly, no.

WARREN: Toby, let it go. Think about *Argo* or something.

TOBY: Oh, man, I can't wait to be in that someday.

WARREN: And you're saying what about me and Josh?

GWEN: I'm sorry, I don't mean to imply anything, I just meant that all couples have issues and I'm sure Lance and Anya are no different, especially during tech week of a show they're both working on—

WARREN: Yeah, but our issues are that Josh is always getting cast better than me. I doubt Lance ever has to worry about losing a part to Anya. Lance never has to worry about losing a part period.

BETTINA: That's because Mr. Monroe runs the company, but in your case, Mr. Alving, it's a matter of Mr. Baker being a significantly better actor than you.

WARREN: He is not that much better than me.

BETTINA: I'm hardly alone in my opinion.

WARREN: Toby?

TOBY: Oh, man, Josh is like Daniel Day Lewis good. You must be so proud to hit that.

WARREN: Oh come on.

TOBY: Oh no worries, you're awesome too.

WARREN: Define "awesome."

TOBY: Like… Robert Burke awesome.

WARREN: He's solid. I'll take it.

GWEN: Who's Robert Burke?

BETTINA: He's no Daniel Day Lewis.

TOBY: He was in *Robocop 3*.

GWEN: Who am I?

TOBY: Um… sort of Amy Adams-ish?

GWEN: (*pleased*) Oooo. Thank you.

WARREN: Do Bettina.

TOBY: Oh, that's easy, Bettina's totally—

BETTINA: You say Helen Mirren or you die five minutes after our final curtain.

TOBY: Helen Mirren. Naturally. (*beat*) Did you know her middle name was Lydia?

BETTINA: Yes. So is mine. We also have the same bone structure.

GWEN: What about the same allergy to sunlight?

> *ROY, JOSH, ELECTRA enter. ROY carries two cases of beer, ELECTRA has coffee.*

ROY: Wassup Bitches, beer is here.

BETTINA: Where have you been?

ELECTRA: Don't talk to me.

BETTINA: Please save your teenage revolt for when we're cast in *Salome* together and answer the question.

ELECTRA: Like, I was getting coffee with Anya, right? Back off.

BETTINA: Speak like an empress or I will rip out your tongue, young lady.

GWEN: Where's Anya?

ELECTRA: She's talking to Lance and Cliff.

GWEN: So Lance is here?

BETTINA: I told you nothing was wrong.

ROY: I don't know. Lance looked very serious.

BETTINA: As a director should look.

WARREN: (*pulling JOSH into his arms*) Hi sexy.

JOSH: Don't snuggle me in costume, you'll get make-up on it.

WARREN: (*inhaling him*) But you smell like sweet delicious cigarettes.

JOSH: Stop it. (*he shakes him off*) Act like a professional.

WARREN: Oh, right, because everyone is acting like such a professional right now.

ROY: (*holding up a bottle of each*) Stella or Crispin, Warren?

WARREN: You know I don't want a fucking Crispin.

ROY: (*handing him a bottle*) Cheers.

GWEN: Electra, when exactly did Lance arrive?

ELECTRA: I don't know. He was waiting out front with Cliff when Anya and I got back from Starbuck's.

GWEN: Did he say anything to you?

ELECTRA: No, but they definitely wanted to be alone because he told me to go in with the boys.

BETTINA: It's probably just a production meeting.

GWEN: A production meeting right before dress is usually not a good thing.

TOBY: No, Gwen, it's an awesome thing. Right now is when they're making those last minute decisions that are gonna take this show to the next level. Lance is like that, you can totally see it in his eyes, he's always thinking, always bringing it all together. He's probably been home all day surrounded by notebooks and ashtrays, listening to the Verve and trying to figure out that thing, you know, that's been keeping us at level four when we need to get to level five. He's gonna walk in here, and he's gonna take us to level five. I can feel it.

JOSH: This is ridiculous. Why haven't we started yet?

WARREN: Josh, loosen up. It's just a rehearsal.

JOSH: Oh, I know. I know it's just a rehearsal. Just a dress rehearsal. But hey, still a rehearsal. And thank God, because if it was a performance you'd probably be stoned.

WARREN: What? Oh come on. I did that once. Once. Why do you always bring that up?

JOSH: Because the fact that it occurred to you to do it once still kind of blows my mind.

WARREN: Please. It was closing night and the show was so simple—

JOSH: It was *Hamlet*.

WARREN: Yeah, but I was playing Laertes.

JOSH: But I was playing Hamlet.

WARREN: Yeah, but you weren't the one who was stoned so who cares?

JOSH: You almost forgot to stab me with the poisoned sword.

WARREN: Oh whatever. I was pausing dramatically.

JOSH: Really, really dramatically.

WARREN: Well you know how time is all relative when you're stoned.

JOSH: I do. Which is why I would never get stoned and then go act in a play.

WARREN: No, you'd just get stoned and try to convince me to fuck you without a condom in the backseat of my car.

JOSH: Once. I did that once. With you. Who I know.

WARREN: It was on our first date and it creeped me out.

JOSH: Well you apparently got over it!

WARREN: THAT'S MY POINT! You don't hold shit against people 'cause they do something stupid once!

JOSH: You don't go on stage on drugs, Warren! You just don't!

WARREN: Even if it was a play you've done a whole lot of times? I mean, if you think the Broadway cast of *Chicago* doesn't go on fucked out of their minds at least once a week, you are dead wrong!

JOSH: That show has been playing forever. Our show was a sixteen performance run!

WARREN: But it was my fourth production of *Hamlet*. Which you know, because you met me during my third production. In which you were also playing Hamlet, and in which I was also playing Laertes! Only you were playing Hamlet for the first time and I was playing Laertes—FOR THE THIRD TIME!

JOSH: It's not my fault you keep getting cast as Laertes!

WARREN: It is when you keep auditioning for the same productions as me!

JOSH: I didn't even know you the first two times!

WARREN: It doesn't matter—you were alive in the world and I haven't had a lead role since you were born!

ANYA: Excuse me, everyone, but could I have your attention please?

Everyone turns from JOSH and WARREN fighting to see ANYA and CLIFF standing at the door of the dressing room. An uncomfortable silence.

ANYA: I'm sure you're all anxious to get the dress rehearsal started, but I'm afraid I have an announcement I need to make first.

BETTINA: Where's Mr. Monroe?

ANYA: He's in the booth going over cues with Candace. (*to Josh*) Josh, are you comfortable staying? Do you want to leave?

JOSH: I'm fine, Anya, thank you.

ANYA: Did you want to say anything?

WARREN: Josh, what's going on?

JOSH: No, I'm good. You say what you need to say.

WARREN: What the fuck is going on?

ANYA: Does Warren know?

WARREN: Know what?

CLIFF: Josh is bailing on us.

WARREN: What?

JOSH: That is not true!

CLIFF: It's the short version.

ANYA: Cliff, I asked you to—

CLIFF: I'm sorry, Anya, but you're gonna try to be nice about it—

JOSH: She's trying to be professional about it, Cliff. You should follow the example.

CLIFF: Excuse me, you pretentious little fag?

JOSH: What?

ANYA: Hey, Cliff, that's not cool—shut up.

JOSH: Yes, please shut up.

ANYA: You too, Josh. (*beat*) Thank you. (*beat*) First of all, I'd like to say I'm sorry we're running so late tonight. There are a couple of things going on that Lance needed to attend to and, as we all know, when tech week hits, whatever can go wrong pretty much always will go wrong. Wait, is this everybody?

CLIFF: Darren and Vic are still on dinner break.

BETTINA: Could we please find out what is going on?

ANYA: I'm sorry, I'm trying to get there. (*beat*) Josh has brought it to my attention that he has been given another opportunity, for which we should all congratulate him. Unfortunately for us, there is a direct conflict with this opportunity and Josh being able to finish the run of the show. Luckily for us, he'll be able to get us through opening weekend, and then we'll have three days to train a replacement.

BETTINA: Has a replacement been found?

ANYA: Yes. That's where Lance was. I'm happy to say Zach Eddelstien has agreed to take on the role. He will start watching rehearsals tomorrow and he'll watch our Friday show and the Sunday matinee. Then if we can get everyone who is in the 1809 scenes to attend some pick-up rehearsals on Monday and Tuesday evenings, we'll do another full dress on Wednesday—provided you can make it of course. I understand you were expecting those three nights off and may have already made other plans, but if you can, of course, move or cancel those plans, please do so.

ELECTRA: I can't be there.

BETTINA: You'll be there.

ELECTRA: Mom!

BETTINA: You will be there, Electra.

ELECTRA: Like, why the fuck do I have to be there when Josh gets to drop out, right?

BETTINA: Mr. Baker is the captain of his own ship. You are still a second class passenger on mine.

ELECTRA: You told me that if I could get Dina to reschedule for the break, I could take the commercial.

BETTINA: Has Dina rescheduled?

ELECTRA: I haven't had a chance to call. I've been here, right, dealing with this shit!

BETTINA: Well now you don't have to call. You are already booked.

JOSH: Oh, let her do the commercial, Bettina. It's clearly what she wants to do and if you really want her to be an actress then it'll get her a lot farther than anything she does here.

ELECTRA: Thank you.

BETTINA: Mr. Baker, though I appreciate your talent and your experience, of course, there are ways to get ahead that are appropriate and ways to get ahead that are not.

JOSH: Sure. Though I don't see why you get to determine that for Electra when it's not exactly like you knew how to get anywhere yourself.

BETTINA: Sir, I have been on the stage of the Royal Shakespeare Company.

JOSH: Yes, but you ended up here.

ANYA: JOSH!

CLIFF: Ended up here.

ROY: Oh, shit.

CLIFF: I fucking knew it.

TOBY: Oh, shit just got real, didn't it?

CLIFF: I knew that it wasn't about your fucking bullshit opportunity.

ROY: Yeah, shit just got way fucking real.

CLIFF: It's about how you have been waiting to take a fucking leak on this place—

JOSH: What the fuck are you talking about?

CLIFF: Oh come on, Josh. Everyone knows you have been kicking for your big break since the day you got here.

JOSH: I have an eye to my future—

CLIFF: No, you're a pretty boy who wants attention, and a bigger venue for that attention, it's not the same thing.

JOSH: Well then you should be happy to get rid of me.

CLIFF: I am happy to get rid of you. I just can't believe that after everything Lance and Anya have done for you—

JOSH: Hey, I am doing my best to be a professional here, okay? I mean, I got them to wait a week for me. I could have have left today, but I didn't.

CLIFF: Oh thank God for the courtesy on their side. When did you audition?

JOSH: What?

CLIFF: When did you audition?

JOSH: Last week.

CLIFF: Okay. Good. And when did you get cast in this show?

JOSH: That doesn't matter.

CLIFF: When did we fill out your fucking Equity paperwork and when did Lance cut the budget for half of your boyfriend's directing project so we could pay you enough that they would let us cast you so you could be in the lead role of a show for the people who helped you get that fucking card in the first place, not to mention took in your never-actually-graduated from Julliard ass when nobody else wanted to cast you because you were real fucking pretty but couldn't act your way out of a bag? When did that happen?

JOSH: I don't know.

CLIFF: February. That's when Josh. February. And that's why you fucking suck, Josh.

JOSH: Look, I didn't think they were actually gonna cast me—

CLIFF: Bullshit. If there's one thing we all know about you, it's that you always think you're going to be cast.

WARREN: That's because you band of fuckwads always cast him. (*Beat.*) Congrats, by the way. When were you planning to tell me? And how? Or is this it, right here?

ANYA: Okay. Everyone on stage. Roy, Electra, Toby—now. Go.

BETTINA: Thank you.

ANYA: Roy, leave the beer.

ROY: Okay.

He chugs it.

ANYA: The one in your pocket too.

ROY: Damn girl.

ANYA: Thank you.

BETTINA: Is my dress done?

ANYA: Yes. I left it in the front row. Cliff can you help her?

CLIFF: Seriously?

ANYA: Yes. And call Darren and Vic please, they should be back by now.

CLIFF: I'll let Lance do it. (*to everyone else*) Come on, everyone.

*EVERYONE but WARREN and JOSH exit. ANYA
lets the others leave before speaking.*

ANYA: I'm giving you two minutes and then Josh I
need you on stage and Warren I need you focused—and
I need you sober. Are we clear? (*they nod agreement;
she turns to go, then turns back*) And I love you both
like my own kids, you know that, and Warren, we cast
Josh because we believe in him every bit as much as we
believe in you, and if he needs to move on we support
that. And I am proud of you, Josh, and happy for you
but, honey, if I were you I would get on your knees and
grovel right now because if Lance ever did to me what
you just did I would divorce him in a heart beat.

JOSH: Outside, you told me I was handling this
professionally.

ANYA: Your boyfriend isn't your co-star, Josh. He's your
boyfriend. Even when you're in a play together.

*She exits. JOSH and WARREN stare at one
another. JOSH doesn't say anything.*

WARREN: The young man waits patiently and refrains
from drinking more.

JOSH: Stop that. It's affected and it makes you sound
autistic.

WARREN: The young man thinks, I've often wondered
if I am autistic.

JOSH: You're not autistic.

WARREN: Would Josh still love me if I was autistic?
Does Josh love me at all?

JOSH: I was going to tell you, I was just very excited. I
only found out this morning.

WARREN: The young man wonders, do autistic people ever wonder if they are not autistic?

JOSH: I know I should have told you I was auditioning, but I didn't think I would get it.

WARREN: Do autistic people ever look at non-autistic people and think, "What the hell is wrong with them? Are they autistic?"

JOSH: If you're not going to listen to me I'm not going to talk to you.

WARREN: So what is it?

JOSH: What?

WARREN: What is this mysterious opportunity?

JOSH: It's a touring production.

WARREN: Of?

JOSH: Why does it matter?

WARREN: Because I want to know.

A long moment.

JOSH: *Fern Gully the Musical.*

Another long moment.

WARREN: Are you one of the fairies or one of the construction workers?

JOSH: I'm one of the fairies.

WARREN: Are you the Christian Slater fairy?

JOSH: That isn't what he's called in the script and you know it.

WARREN: You're right. I don't want to know.

JOSH: Fine. We'll talk after rehearsal.

JOSH starts to exit but WARREN lunges and grabs him, spinning him around so they are face to face.

WARREN: Look at my fucking eyes.

JOSH: What the fuck, Warren—!

WARREN: LOOK AT MY FUCKING EYES. (*beat*) What do you see?

JOSH: What? You're upset?

WARREN: I'm upset?

JOSH: I don't understand what you want me to see!

WARREN: My eye-liner is the most perfect it has ever been, Josh. THE MOST PERFECT. IT HAS EVER. BEEN. (*beat; he lets him go*) And you are not going to fuck that up for me.

A long moment. They look at one another. WARREN straightens his costume and exits. JOSH stands there, frozen. GWEN enters.

GWEN: Josh, they need you on stage.

JOSH nods. He straightens his own costume and heads to the door. He turns back.

JOSH: Nobody here ever really liked me anyway.

He exits. The lights fade on GWEN.

SCENE TWO: OPENING

In the dark we hear a champagne cork pop.
The lights come up to reveal the dressing room.
TOBY, ROY, BETTINA, GWEN, WARREN and
ELECTRA. They are in their own clothes, but
everyone still has make-up on. Champagne, wine,
beer. On one side of the room, TOBY is talking
to ROY and ELECTRA. On the other side of the
room, BETTINA is talking to GWEN. WARREN
sits in the middle, drinking directly from a bottle
of wine.

TOBY: So you know that ending sequence where the shit really hits the fan?

BETTINA: Electra's birth, of course, is the greatest single achievement of my life.

TOBY: It fucking kills me every time. Like, okay, right, the Important Native American dude has just told Danny Day he can go free, but they're gonna kill Madeline Stowe while the Beautiful Girl has been given to the Evil Native American dude so he can get her pregnant right? And then the Blonde Guy who you were pretty certain was a douche suddenly sacrifices himself so Stowe can make a break for it with Danny Day and the Old Native American dude, whose son is in love with the Beautiful Girl. And that's the first moment you're just damn—these are complicated fucking people.

BETTINA: My husband and I were still living in England at the time, and while I wouldn't say I was exactly the leading lady of the RSC, I certainly had attained an enviable place in the company, having played Paulina the previous season, and then Beatrice earlier that year.

TOBY: And it just keeps getting better, right, because you're jump cutting between all these really beautiful shots of the world which is just pristine cause it's the past, you know, and all the Native American dudes are walking on a cliff and there's waterfalls and they're getting away with the Beautiful Girl and suddenly BAM, the Young Native American dude steps out and just starts kicking ass and you're like, I knew it was gonna happen man, I knew they were gonna save the Beautiful Girl because they had to. But then the Evil Native American dude kills the Young Native American dude. And that's when you're just like shit—life is not fucking fair.

BETTINA: And then I got the news and it was so… devastating and terrifying at the same time. I was, of course, elated, but you must understand how unsettling such a thing is when you are on a steady upward ascent, feeling there is a real plan you're following, and then to have such a huge, important, life-changing event thrust upon you, even when it was something you had been hoping for. Of course I had always said to myself, "In due time Bettina, all in due time" and then all of a sudden it was time.

TOBY: So the cuts keep jumping and the music is getting so intense, you know, and that's when the fucking shit really hits the fan. Danny Day and Madeline and the Old Native American dude are all running through those amazing trees in that world we're never gonna get back again, right, and then it cuts back to the Evil Native American dude and the Beautiful Girl steps away from him and up onto the ledge of the ravine and that's when you're like, this is going to just eviscerate me, isn't it?

BETTINA: And God was she beautiful. So powerful, right from the beginning, so strong and yet so vulnerable, so demanding of the best I had to give the world. And I blossomed under that demand, I assure you, once I understood how much would be required of me, for I knew this is what I had been intended for and that this would be the crowning moment of my life: bringing her into the world, creating her inside me and then introducing her to the light. This is what I had been intended for by Fate. By God.

TOBY: And God she is so beautiful, you know? Like those final few frames of her face, against the huge endless sky, and her hair and the rags of her dress floating around her in the breeze, the sprinkling of rain, just the tiniest touch of it, like a cloud is passing over just her, and the look on her face. The absolute confidence she has in that final moment, once she knows what she's going to do and how it hits you, just as it hits the Evil Dude, and he lowers his knife and begs her to come back from the edge but she just turns and walks off and you're like fuck, art is fucking amazing.

BETTINA: It was an astounding eight weeks of sold out performances and the kind of reviews you dream of getting. I was compared to Sarah Bernhardt, Vivien Leigh, Cate Blanchett. We extended six weeks and I would have done the tour if I hadn't gotten pregnant. But I suppose Fate wanted my star to burn as brief as it was bright because suddenly it was goodbye crown and chiton, hello motherhood and fading obscurity.

TOBY: Then you get the final show down between the Old Native American and the Evil One, and Danny Day and Madeline are together, but it's so bittersweet, right, because everyone's dead and the Old Native is like the last of his tribe. And you get that final moment where they all look out over the pristine world they haven't even begun to explore yet and it really brings home how we're all, at some point, going to end, everything is going to end, and so you have to just fucking seize it, you know?

BETTINA: Terrence wanted to name her something awful like Nancy but I insisted Electra be christened with the name of my true daughter.

TOBY: And that's when I knew I wanted to be an actor.

BETTINA: Of course, I suppose that makes me Clytemnestra, doesn't it?

A long moment in both conversations.

GWEN: Wow, that was just...

ELECTRA: Excuse me...

GWEN: I am gonna open another bottle of champagne.

ELECTRA: I need to refill my glass.

ELECTRA and GWEN both slip away from the conversations they were in.

TOBY: Dude, you think she's kind of hot?

ROY: No.

ANYA and CLIFF enter.

ANYA: I thought it was a great show. A very strong opening.

CLIFF: I thought the last sound cue was a bit soft. I'll tell Candace to bump it up for the matinee tomorrow.

ANYA: I didn't think it was too much of a problem.

CLIFF: No, it was fine. Just could have been louder. I'll tell Candace to make it louder.

ANYA: Don't tell her tonight. Let her enjoy the party.

CLIFF: I can't believe people are still sticking around.

ANYA: Free champagne is free champagne.

CLIFF: Yeah, but Dear God is that a long play.

ANYA: I don't think it's that bad.

CLIFF: It's almost three and a half hours of people talking around a table.

ANYA: Still feels shorter than *Red Light Winter*.

GWEN and ELECTRA encounter each other over a bottle of champagne.

GWEN: Hey.

ELECTRA: Hey.

GWEN: Are you allowed to be having this?

ELECTRA: It's good champagne and this is an opening party so like, my mother doesn't really care, right? She'd only flip a bitch if I was guzzling box wine in the bathroom at school or something.

GWEN: Well, I thought you did very well tonight, so you definitely deserve some champagne.

ELECTRA: Yeah, it was a good show. Which was kind of surprising, right?

GWEN: Not too surprising, I think.

ELECTRA: Eh. I guess I'm just not really into this show. It's really long.

GWEN: It is, but… I mean, I like it, I guess. I'm sorry we don't have any scenes together.

ELECTRA: Whatever. All the women's roles in this play are kind of bogus. Like, I know this Stoppard guy is a big deal or whatever, but I don't think it's some kind of massive achievement because he has a girl doing math. If he really gave a crap about her as a character he could give her more lines instead of spending most of the play focusing on the piss-fights between the eggheads and then having her moon over the biggest egghead of the bunch. Who is like, kind of creepy.

GWEN: You think Septimus is creepy?

ELECTRA: Any character who fucks a character played by my mom is creepy, right?

ANYA joins BETTINA.

BETTINA: Did you get a chance to talk to Zach?

ANYA: No, but Lance said he'll be at the matinee tomorrow.

BETTINA: I'm worried he won't have time to memorize the lines.

ANYA: Zach's always been a quick study. We're very lucky he was available. Young men of his caliber are not easy to come by on short notice.

BETTINA: They certainly are not. I must admit, I'm sorry to see Josh go though.

ANYA: It's an excellent opportunity for him.

BETTINA: I know, but… He makes a good Septimus.

ANYA: He'll make a good fairy too.

BETTINA: I didn't even know he could sing.

CLIFF joins ROY and TOBY.

CLIFF: Good opening, everyone.

ROY: Toby wants to stick it in Electra.

TOBY: I did not say that!

CLIFF: Nigga that is fucking sick.

ROY: Shit, Toby you just shocked the Black back into Cliff!

CLIFF: Fuck you, Roy.

ROY: Oh don't act like you don't want it.

TOBY: If Electra's too young for me, she's way too young for Cliff.

ROY: Not Cuntasina, Little T, I'm talking about my panny pudding.

CLIFF: It's really impossible to say which of those ideas is more appalling to me.

TOBY: What's panny pudding?

ELECTRA is scrolling through her phone while GWEN keeps trying to talk to her.

GWEN: Well, I still think Thomasina is a wonderful part for someone your age.

ELECTRA: Yeah, that's what my mom said. But I've had way better.

TOBY: (*shouting from across the room*) OH MY GOD THAT'S DISGUSTING!

GWEN: What's your favorite role that you've played?

ELECTRA: In theater? I don't know. Mary Lennox?

GWEN: That's a good role.

ELECTRA: (*texting the whole time*) Yeah, well, and unlike every other young girl in theater nobody like… rapes her or tries to rape her, right? I mean, I was Wendela—raped. I was Wendela in the musical—seduced by an idiot which is as good as raped, right? I was Miranda—almost raped. I was Imogen—almost raped. I was Alice—raped. I was Polyxena—raped and killed. I was Lavinia—raped and maimed. And then killed. I was in *The Europeans* and I got raped by the Turks. I was in a kid's version of *Les Mis* and got raped by all of France. I was Agnes and I got raped by God. I was Louisa and got raped by poetry or some shit. Last year I did *The Vagina Monologues* and that was like Rape City, right? I bet Septimus wants to rape Thomasina. He's definitely way too interested in her for an old guy. Mom's dream role for me is Salome and in that play, her step-dad wants to rape her until he realizes she's too fucked up even for him. I know theater people are like, so convinced Hollywood is sleaze, but like, I've been in six commercials and three television shows and I've never once had to play a kid who got raped or might get raped. Like, you don't sell Kashi with a raped kid, right? But I swear, every time I get a call for a stage show, it's some creepy role in some creepy play where some creepy guy wants to molest me. And my mom says that's just how it's gonna be until I'm old enough to play queens.

GWEN: You know, I want to contradict that… but all I can think about is how the roles I got in college were Isabella in *Measure of Measure*, Lady Anne in *Richard III* and Terry in *Extremeties*.

ELECTRA: They get raped?

GWEN: Sort of?

ELECTRA: See, theater is stupid. I don't get why people do it. But I really don't get why women do it, right? I mean, there's like no roles to begin with, and half of the roles involve you getting raped, or trying not to get raped. And yes, I know rape is important and we should talk about it, but hello, is this really why I had to get all those headshots done? Like none of which show me getting raped, right? (*She looks up from her phone.*) So what do you think Toby's deal is?

GWEN: Excuse me?

ELECTRA: I mean he's sort of cute, right?

GWEN: I'm afraid all I can think about right now is how many creepy men out there have copies of my headshots.

> *CLIFF has been explaining "panny pudding" to TOBY.*

CLIFF: And that's more or less what it tastes like, yeah.

TOBY: Wow. Man. That is some fucked up shit.

ROY: Hazzard of the trade, homie. When you dig for gold in holy crevice, it's just a hazzard of the trade.

TOBY: Man, I am just never gonna do that.

ROY/CLIFF: Your loss.

TOBY: I mean, why would you when the other way is just so much easier?

ROY: Just feels really good.

CLIFF: I'm not into ladyparts.

TOBY: Which makes sense, now, but I had no idea that straight people—

CLIFF: Oh, sure, lots of them do it.

TOBY: Really?

ROY: Bet you Danny Day does.

CLIFF: You know, he probably does.

TOBY: That's crazy. (*beat*) Is it really that good?

ROY/**CLIFF:** Yup.

ROY: And some bitches really like it. Like really really like it.

TOBY: They do?

ROY/CLIFF: Oh yeah.

TOBY: You think Electra's into that?

    ROY and CLIFF exchange looks.

ROY: Fuck yeah, motherfucker!

CLIFF: Talks about it all time.

ROY: All those English bitches like it that way.

CLIFF: Science fact.

ROY: That's where Danny Day learned it.

TOBY: In England?

ROY: Damn straight. Right Cliff?

CLIFF: Absolutely. Probably on like… the set of *A Room With A View*.

TOBY: Wow. (*beat*) But she doesn't even have an English accent. Does that still count?

ROY: Sure does.

CLIFF: Absolutely.

JOSH enters. He is not wearing any make-up.

JOSH: Hey everybody.

Everyone turns and looks at JOSH, except for WARREN. A moment, then ANYA leaps into action.

ANYA: Hey, Josh, great show! Great opening!

JOSH: Thanks, Anya. You too.

ANYA: Do you want some wine? Some champagne?

JOSH: Champagne sounds great.

ANYA: Cliff, could you—?

CLIFF: No.

ROY: I got it.

ROY brings a bottle and a glass over to JOSH.

JOSH: Thanks.

ROY: No problem, buddy. Good show.

JOSH: Good show.

GWEN: We were wondering where you were.

BETTINA: We assumed the general awkwardness had sent you home early.

JOSH: I wanted to get my make-up off, thank you.

ROY: Understood, homeboy. Nothing's worse than passing out drunk with a face full of crunk.

JOSH: You said it.

ANYA: Actually, we really shouldn't all be hiding in the dressing room. Lance is out there with a lobby full of people and I'm sure he could use some help—

JOSH: I don't think he really wants to see me.

CLIFF: What, and you think we do?

ANYA: Cliff, do you need to be cut off?

CLIFF: You can't cut me off yet, I'm nowhere near drunk enough to consider throwing a punch or smashing a bottle over someone's head.

ANYA: And congratulations, you are officially cut off.

CLIFF: Whatever.

ANYA: No really, Cliff. Go home. Or go hang out in the lobby.

CLIFF: But I'm so comfortable here.

ANYA: Cliff!

JOSH: It's okay, Anya. I will go home. I actually have a whole lot of packing to do. I just wanted to stop in and say goodnight to everyone. And good show. Really. It's been an honor to work with you all.

ANYA: Josh, stay.

JOSH: Thanks. But I don't exactly feel welcome.

ANYA: It's your last opening with us. I would really like you to stay.

JOSH: I'm sure it's not my last.

WARREN: But it probably is. (*turning to him*) So you should stay.

JOSH: If I do, will you talk to me?

WARREN: I can not promise you anything. (*beat*) But you should stay. If you want to.

A moment.

JOSH: Then I will.

Another moment.

ROY: Okay, anyone want to go smoke some weed outside?

CLIFF: Abso-fucking-lutely.

ROY: Toby?

TOBY: Yeah. Electra?

ELECTRA: Sure.

BETTINA: Stay right where you are, young lady.

ELECTRA: I'm just going outside, Mom, I wasn't, like, gonna do anything.

TOBY: You weren't? What's the point then?

ROY: Homie, you got no fucking game.

CLIFF: None.

ELECTRA: They're right, you're pathetic.

TOBY: Are you into that?

GWEN: It's okay, Bettina, I'll keep her out of trouble.

BETTINA: I appreciate the offer, Miss Howard, but I'm afraid the governess who can keep Electra in line has yet to be born.

GWEN: Did you just call me a governess?

CLIFF: Get used to it, New Girl, took her three years to stop calling me "boy."

ROY: Really?

CLIFF: Yup.

ROY: Negro, that's some fucked up shit.

CLIFF: Word.

ANYA: You know, I think we could all use some fresh air—let's all go outside, huh? Maybe break bottles in the street or something. Let off some steam.

ROY: (*excited*) Seriously?

ANYA: No, Roy. Bettina? Some air?

BETTINA: Some air would be lovely. The theater was so stuffy.

ANYA: I'm sure we're all tired of being in the theater.

ELECTRA: That's fucking true.

BETTINA: She's talking about this specific theater, on this specific day, Electra.

ELECTRA: Oh. Right.

ANYA: And maybe we could all stop in at the lobby? Say hello to the Board?

CLIFF: God, I definitely need to be stoned for that.

ELECTRA: No kidding.

ANYA: People, it's your job as actors to mingle. I need you to mingle.

BETTINA: And mingle we shall.

ANYA: Thank you.

BETTINA: But we're still keeping the good champagne in here. This isn't *Miss Julie*.

They all drift out except for JOSH and WARREN. A moment.

JOSH: You sure you don't want to go get stoned? We could get seriously baked and have rough, nasty sex in the booth.

WARREN: I'm already pretty fucked up, thank you.

JOSH: It's been barely an hour since the show ended.

WARREN: You of all people know, I can do anything when I put my mind to it. (*he waves the wine bottle*) This is my second one. And this is not quality wine.

JOSH: Why do you do this to yourself?

WARREN: You know why. You do know why, don't you?

JOSH: You're gonna end up puking.

WARREN: I like vomitting. I always feel clean afterwards.

JOSH: Gross.

WARREN: Yeah. I'm disgusting.

JOSH: Sometimes. (*beat*) We need to sort some stuff out.

WARREN: Understatement.

JOSH: I mean, there are some practical things. That we should have sorted out a few days ago, but... you wouldn't talk to me.

WARREN: I'm sorry. I feel betrayed.

JOSH: I get that, but I am leaving on Monday for five months and I need to know stuff.

WARREN: Like?

JOSH: Like… do you want my car and how do you want to pay bills? Should I leave you some money or do you want to just have me keep putting money into the account? Should I put stuff in storage? Do I have a place when I come back or… or is this over? (*beat*) Is this over?

WARREN: I don't… okay, um… sure… and don't worry about it we'll call the car mine and it'll be a wash and yes, I guess, probably you should store stuff, but if there isn't time I can do it for you and, no, I don't know, but… maybe. Probably. Don't you feel like it is?

JOSH: It doesn't have to be. I mean, I'm not going forever, I'm coming back—

WARREN: Are you sure of that? Can you promise that? I mean what if the tour extends. What if it goes to Europe? What if they make a musical of *Fern Gully 2* and they want you to be in that too? I mean, we both know that you would say yes—

JOSH: Look, let's not make any decisions here, okay?

WARREN: You said you needed to know stuff.

JOSH: I know, but… I was wrong. Let's just play it by ear, okay?

WARREN: Okay. I didn't realize we had such a casual relationship but you know—

JOSH: I just mean let's leave things open and not add stress to this… this moment. Though, while we're on it… sure. Maybe we need to recognize that we're going to be apart for at least almost half a year and if something happens, or we meet someone—

WARREN: I'm not really going to be looking for a new boyfriend anytime soon—

JOSH: I just mean, if we sleep with someone or whatever we don't beat up ourselves or each other or… or rule anything out. I mean, we're both young, stuff happens—

WARREN: Yeah, it happens when you let it happen.

JOSH: Let's not be prudes, is all I'm saying. I mean, we've both fucked around—

WARREN: What?

JOSH: Oh come on. We've both slept with Cliff—

WARREN: You slept with Cliff?

JOSH: Didn't you?

WARREN: No.

JOSH: I mean… I thought that you knew. Why do you think he's such a dick to me?

WARREN: I don't know, I just always figured you deserved it. (*beat*) Are you excited?

JOSH: About?

WARREN: About? Really?

JOSH: Oh. Right. Sure.

WARREN: That's not very convincing.

JOSH: Of course I'm excited.

WARREN: You should be. You always said this is what you always wanted to do—

JOSH: Well, I never said touring was really what I wanted to—

WARREN: No. You didn't. In fact you used to say you thought touring sounded pretty fucking awful.

JOSH: Yeah, well, that was before I started to feel like going nowhere was pretty fucking awful.

WARREN: Sounds pretty fucking awful. (*beat*) You weren't going nowhere.

JOSH: I wasn't going somewhere fast enough. (*beat*) Look, I know this is not ideal, and that I really fucked up here, but... but this is all I want to do with my life, and probably the only thing I am actually any good at and... and so I know I have to take this chance. I have to. Please. Warren. Understand that for me? I have to try while I still can. If only so I can know if there ever was any kind of chance to... I mean... Please. I have to try. Before it's too late and I'm too... old.

WARREN: You're still young.

JOSH: I won't always be. (*beat*) And neither will you.

WARREN: I know. I know that. Do you think... I don't know that?

JOSH: Look, I'm not like you, Warren.

WARREN: That's why I like you, Josh.

JOSH: This is where you belong, but it's not where I belong.

WARREN: What?

JOSH: This, here. All this here. With Lance and Anya—

WARREN: Don't say anything shitty about Lance and Anya.

JOSH: It's not saying something shitty about them. I'm

just saying that I want more than this. That's not saying something shitty to say that. They understand that. I want more.

WARREN: And you don't think I do?

JOSH: No. No, I don't… always… I don't think you do.

WARREN: Of course I do. Of course I fucking do, Josh. But wanting more doesn't mean I look down on this place or the people who have helped me do great work here—

JOSH: I don't look down on this place, I really don't, I wish people would stop saying—

WARREN: More importantly, Josh, wanting more does not mean being willing to do or be anything that is required of me simply so I can climb rungs or some fucking ladder that I have no proof even leads anywhere—

JOSH: You make it sound like I'm selling out just because I'm taking a gig—

WARREN: Well you kind of are selling out—

JOSH: A touring production of a Broadway show is a pretty respectable gig—

WARREN: Not when it's a fucking family entertainment musical and based on a cartoon and basically engineered to pander to the broadest swatch of mediocrity and suck money from anyone with children—who you hate, by the way, so you can't even tell me you're doing it for the kids—and hello you're not even playing a human being!

JOSH: I wasn't when I played Oberon either.

WARREN: Do not try to compare *A Midsummer Night's Dream* with *Fern Gully the Musical*!

JOSH: What do you want me to say? That it's a piece of fluff? Fine, it's a piece of fluff.

WARREN: It's a piece of shit, Josh—which wouldn't actually matter, if it wasn't for the part where I know you also think it's a piece of shit.

JOSH: Who the fuck even cares what the show is?

WARREN: I do! I do every time! That's the first question I ask myself when I consider auditioning or consider directing or consider buying a ticket! I ask, "what is the show?" and that usually leads to "why is the show?" and "why me and this show?" and "what does it teach me?" and "what do I do with what I learn?" and "how do I live now" and all that answers "why does it matter?" and "it" might be the show and "it" might be life itself, the point of fucking life, my life, your life, our life together, which is the point of fucking art and the point of why I fucking do this! All because of "what is the show?" and not because of "where does it get me?" or "how many points do I get?" or "what does it pay?"

JOSH: Those are all legitimate questions.

WARREN: Yeah, Josh, they are, they absolutely are, but they should be the secondary questions.

JOSH: According to who?

WARREN: According to me! And, I thought, you.

JOSH: Why did you think that?

WARREN: Because I'm fucking stupid that way, Josh. Because I'm fucking dumb.

JOSH: You're not dumb. You're not stupid. But I will say, you'd probably be a lot farther along with your career by now if some of those questions were more important to you.

WARREN: And there, at last, is the point.

JOSH: What? No. This is a real opportunity, a real chance for me to be a real actor—

WARREN: Cause what we do here isn't real is it? (*pause*) Is it?

JOSH: I didn't say that.

WARREN: Yes, you did.

JOSH: I didn't say that what we do here isn't real.

WARREN: You just said that. You just literally said that.

JOSH: I didn't mean it the way you think I do.

WARREN: Well then how did you mean it?

JOSH: I meant it the way people mean it when they say things like that—

WARREN: What kind of people?

JOSH: What do you mean what kind of people?

WARREN: I mean I wouldn't say something like that, so I have to assume you must be talking about some other kind of people, some kind of people who would say something like that, maybe someone like you? I don't know. What kind of person are you?

JOSH: What kind of person am I?

WARREN: Yes, Josh, what kind of person are you?

JOSH: You know what kind of person I am.

WARREN: Really? Do I? That is the question, isn't it? The Big Question: To Be Josh or Not To Be Josh.

JOSH: Oh fuck you.

WARREN: Whether 'tis nobler in the eye of the world to suffer for your art as Warren does or to suffer for you art as Josh does: to be kicked, repeatedly but to retain a smile or to grimly set one's mouth in a line of determination and assume the kicking stance, not because one should but because one has to for one's own career, alas, alack, cruel world, cruel world, cruel world, but it's the one we live in and so must it be, and so must one be if one is to be anything that is real.

JOSH: Fuck you, Warren. Fuck you. Fuck you. Fuck you.

WARREN: Yes, Josh, very articulate, Shakespeare has clearly rubbed off on you.

JOSH: Look, I'm trying to talk to you, but if you keep interrupting with this bullshit—

WARREN: I KEEP INTERRUPTING YOU BECAUSE YOU KEEP TRYING TO HURT ME AND CONTRARY TO WHAT YOU THINK, YOU TREMENDOUS ASSHOLE, I DO NOT HAVE TO ACCEPT YOUR TREATMENT OF ME!

JOSH: I AM NOT TRYING TO HURT YOU—I FUCKING LOVE YOU!

WARREN: REALLY? WELL THAT'S TOO BAD! That's really too bad. Because I still pretty much love you. I love you so much I can look past all the stupid shit you say and do because I can see that scared little boy who is so certain, so deep down certain, that he's never going to go anywhere and I can feel sorry for that guy and that keeps me warm in your direction even as you force yourself to be a dick because you think that is your only option. But the truth of the matter is you're so self-absorbed that you can't realize how you just negated not only my whole life, but my whole life with you… and I can no longer think of single fucking reason to ever speak to you again. And I'm not going to.

JOSH: Warren—

WARREN: No. No. No. We're done here. We're done here, Josh. We're done.

JOSH: Okay. We're done.

A long moment. They look at one another. JOSH reaches out to touch WARREN, but he stops him. Another moment. JOSH nods. WARREN nods back. JOSH exits. WARREN waits for him to go, and then he chugs the entire remainder of the bottle of wine before tossing it into a nearby recycling bin. He sits down on a chair, then lurches to the floor where he spits up a puddle of red wine. A long moment and then:

WARREN: The young man remembers it was his birthday. (*beat*) Happy Birthday, Warren.

CLIFF enters.

CLIFF: Are you okay?

WARREN: It's not blood.

CLIFF: What?

WARREN: The puddle there it's… it's not blood. It's just wine. (*standing up*) I spilled it. I mean, I kind of puked it up but… it was only in there for a few seconds. Like, inside of me. So it's not like… full-on puke.

CLIFF: What are you talking about?

WARREN: I didn't want you to think I'm hurt. (*beat*) I'll clean it up. I know where the mops are. I just pretend I don't because I'm… an overgrown child.

CLIFF: Don't worry about it. Why don't you just go home?

WARREN: Yeah, I probably should. Did Josh—?

CLIFF: He's gone.

WARREN: (*after a moment*) How did he look?

CLIFF: Not great. He was crying.

WARREN: You know he can do that on command, right? It's one of his dog tricks. In the right light it's almost believable.

CLIFF: (*gently, one hand on WARREN's arm*) I really think you should go home.

WARREN: (*he puts his hand on CLIFF's other arm*) What are you gonna do?

CLIFF: I am going to clean up your mess, and then I'm going to kick everybody out, and then I'm going to go home too.

WARREN: (*slipping his hand from CLIFF's arm to his chest*) Alone?

CLIFF: Alone. (*gently*) You're in a dark scary place, Warren. Don't go to a darker, scarier one.

WARREN: (*letting CLIFF go*) Good advice. Very good advice. (*He heads over to one of the tables, and retrieves* *a bag stored underneath. He turns to CLIFF.*) I'll see you tomorrow, Cliff.

CLIFF: See you tomorrow. (*WARREN heads towards the door.*) If you go out the stage door, you won't run into anyone. (*They look at one another.*) Just saying. I mean, that's what it's there for.

> *WARREN exits without answering. CLIFF grabs a roll of paper towels from a nearby make-up table and cleans up the puddle of wine as the lights fade to black.*

SCENE THREE: STRIKE

The dressing room, the day after the last performance. Everywhere we see the remnants of the play: props, costumes, make-up, furnishings, bits of scenery, fabric, curtains, wigs, etc. Also boxes, many boxes, into which all these things are being packed and continue to be packed by various characters throughout the act until the dressing room is completely clean. On one side, ROY and TOBY are putting things away. On the other side, CLIFF and GWEN are working.

CLIFF: Like most people in the theater, I got into this because I thought I wanted to be an actor.

ROY: I don't know, man, personally, I think in the end you gotta define for yourself what success is.

CLIFF: But you know, that dream got beaten out of me in college. Not by anyone in particular, mind you, though we did have one of those faculties whose teaching philosophy was, "the best way to make the cream rise to the top is by telling the milk how terrible it is as often as possible." My problem was more that somewhere along the way, I had become somebody who really cared about my dignity. And the truth is, I'm pretty sure you can't be a great actor if you care too much about your dignity.

ROY: Listen, Little T, I been everywhere a motherfucker can go and still not be famous. I been on TV. I been in student films. I been in independent films. I been on HBO. I been in one super big fucking movie where I brought Meryl Streep a sandwich and she was like, "Thanks" and I was like, "You're welcome" and I got paid a stupid amount of money for that shit. I been in every level of theater you can think of since I was six and played one of those little kids in the *King and I*. I understudied at the Rep, and I went on at the Rep. I got my card. I was in another show at the Rep, this time as part of the cast right from the beginning. And that show went to Broadway and I went with it.

CLIFF: There was this incident—the turning point, if you will—during my sophomore year. I was in *Gem of the Ocean*. Now, I love August Wilson, make no mistake, *Fences* is a masterpiece, but that play... that play leaves a lot to be desired, in my opinion. Still, we're doing it and I'm young and happy to be there, like everybody else, and sure there was a part of me that kept thinking, "Man this is awesome!" But there was also this part of me that kept going "hmmmmmmmm" all through the rehearsal period. Hmmmmmmmmm. Hmmmmmmmm.

ROY: In New York, I worked a lot—enough to pay my rent. My favorite gig ever, though, was in the opera, 'cause people in the theater are cray, but people in the opera are fucking super-cray with a little more cray on top plus they sing. And those bitches work hard and they party hard too. I did more blow when I was in the opera chorus than I ever done in my life and I was fucking twenty-five, worked out and straight: bitches was all over me. But after a while, it got old, like everything does, and I gave it all up and moved back here cause I realized the only thing I really wanted to do with my life was tell stories in different kinds of funny accents.

CLIFF: On opening night, we're knee deep in the big soul cleansing scene that is the climax of the show, this big Voodoo ceremony where everyone's on stage shaking bones and feathers at each other and the lights are spooky blacklights and all the furniture is glowing and my character is going into this big regression and I'm getting there, I really am, when all of a sudden I freeze. At a moment when I am definitely not supposed to be frozen. And then I start laughing. At a moment when I am definitely not supposed to be laughing. And I can't stop. I really want to, of course, because I know I am ruining the play, I can see it on the faces of my fellow actors, and I can see it on the faces of the first three rows of the audience… but I can't. I can't stop.

ROY: Homie, you know what a Pastorella is?

CLIFF: I had heard this voice in my head, and that voice was mine. As in me, Cliff Samuel. And the voice had said, "Voodoo is bullshit." And then another voice had answered that voice back. And that was the voice of my character—whose name I can't even remember now—and my character had answered, "I agree."

ROY: A Pastorella is like a specific type of story, right, that takes place in the countryside, or some place that just ain't where all the action's happening, right, cause everyone is all bucolic and shit and laying around eating grapes and holding shepherd's hooks, tweaking each other's nipples while cherubs dance around with scarves. And like, nothing really happens in these stories—like maybe some motherfucker whose got a lot of goats falls in love with some 'ho who has flowers in her hair, and there's some hi-jinks of the easy-to-resolve kind but these bitches don't got a lot going on. They're not famous, they're not rich, they're not looking to be famous or rich. They're just trying to be happy and love each other and smell the shit out of those fucking roses, you know? Which is why they live in the Pastorella and not the Urbarella, get me?

CLIFF: I got hauled into the head of the department's office the next day and she reamed me one good—and I deserved it. I had fucked up big time. Amazingly, they let me finish the run, but nobody cast me in a lead the rest of my college life—if they cast me at all. And the truth is: I did not mind. I started taking design courses and I liked those a lot more—you could make fun of the actors while still showing them how much you loved them, you know? I like stage management the best because I believe in what actors do and I like being a part of that but I don't buy what actors do and in order to be a good actor you got to buy into it. And I just can't do that. Because it's all Voodoo in the end, if you ask me. And I don't believe in God and I don't believe in magic and I definitely don't believe in Voodoo. I just love seeing the looks on the faces of people who do.

ROY: The fact is, I made it to the Urbarella, and I made it in the Urbarella, and I looked around, and I thought, "All I really want is the Pastorella." Cause like, life was fun and crazy and all, but the fact is, I wasn't doing much special. I wasn't telling stories. I was playing small parts, mostly, and the majority of the people I knew was in the same position: playing bit parts, being in the chorus, being an understudy, maybe going on now and then. But not like, getting their voice out there. Never center stage. Black, white, yellow, young, old, male, female, pretty, ugly… didn't matter. Barely a star amongst. Barely an opportunity to be a star. Let alone an artist. And after a while, it started to feel a lot like a job. A job I liked, yeah, but I thought about it, and I thought,

"Fuck, I can think of like twenty other jobs I'd like that pay a lot better than this shit... and probably still do this shit and get better parts." So when my last show in New York closed, I packed my shit and went home, auditioned for shit, got offered the lead in the *King and I* over at the Light Opera Palace, and found out I couldn't do it and keep my card. So I gave up the card and now I'm here with all of you and aside from having to play the occasional bullshit butler role, I'm pretty happy. Especially as Warren just cast my ass as Mercutio.

TOBY: Who is Mercutio?

ROY: The best fucking role in that whole fucking play.

TOBY: What play?

ROY: Seriously? That's pathetic. Open a book, asshole.

ANYA comes in with several plastic tubs.

ANYA: It looks like we have everything off the stage. Cliff, do you have everything shut down in the booth and put away?

CLIFF: I need to do a quick sweep but yeah, I think so.

ANYA: You want to do that now, and then Lance can lock the theater and maybe you can head over to your place, finish getting ready for the party?

CLIFF: Yeah, if you don't think you'll need me.

ANYA: No, I'd say you can go. Roy, you probably can too, if you want.

ROY: Fuck to the yeah. You want some help, Cliff? I stack a mean charcoal pyramid.

CLIFF: Nobody touches my grill but me. You can wash stuff.

ROY: Sweet. I call shot-gun.

CLIFF: You don't need to call it when there's only two of us in the car and I'm driving. (*to ANYA*) You're sure an hour? 'Cause if I get that grill going and you are all still here you know it's going to make me cry and nobody wants to see that happen again.

ANYA: Hour. Hour-and-a-half, tops.

CLIFF: Call me when you're actually leaving. Come on, Roy.

> *CLIFF and ROY exit, passing ELECTRA as she enters, carrying a gym bag on one shoulder. She seems oddly nervous.*

ELECTRA: Has anyone seen my make-up case?

ROY: We took a dump in it and then hid it. You're welcome.

ELECTRA: Fuck off, Roy. (*to CLIFF*) Hey, you're gonna have vegan food at this party, right?

CLIFF: Yes.

ELECTRA: Thank you. Mom was all like, "Nobody is going cater to your freakish diet, Electra," and I was all like, "Mother, please, just because Cliff is Black doesn't mean he doesn't know his way around the vegetable section of the grocery store, right?"

CLIFF: Dear God, you are both just terrible, aren't you?

ELECTRA: Anyway, see you there.

CLIFF: See you there.

> *CLIFF and ROY exit. ELECTRA starts looking around the room.*

ELECTRA: I know I left it somewhere in here, right? I mean, I thought I had put it in the car, but like I guess I didn't because I couldn't find it this morning and there's like, nowhere else it could be, right?

ANYA: We missed you at strike.

ELECTRA: I'm sorry, I had an audition.

ANYA: For what?

ELECTRA: Another cereal commercial. I swear, it's like all people want to do is watch me eat whole grains.

ANYA: Do you think you got it?

ELECTRA: Probably. Nobody can fake a smile with their mouth full like me, right? (*she sees the make-up case*) Oh! Found it! (*she pulls a make-up case out from under a table; a moment as she considers it, then turns to TOBY*) Hey, um... Tony...

TOBY: Toby.

ELECTRA: Right. Would you mind, like... just... opening this for me.

TOBY: Sure. (*He takes the case from her, places it on the table and opens it.*) What now?

ELECTRA: Look in it.

TOBY: And?

ELECTRA: What do you see?

TOBY: Make-up.

ELECTRA: Oh good. I was kind of actually worried.

TOBY: About?

ELECTRA: Forget it. I was being stupid. (*She hurriedly* *closes the box and picks it up, stuffing it into her gym bag; at the same time she discretely places an envelope on the table)* Like, nobody is that gross, right? Not even Roy. *(beat)* Well, see you at the party?

TOBY: Yeah. You?

ELECTRA: Sure.

She starts to go.

TOBY: Hey!

She turns.

ELECTRA: Yeah?

TOBY: Um… I was just thinking… I mean, I don't know if you'd ever want to like… you know.

ELECTRA: Like… you know… what?

TOBY: Like… I mean, I'm not like… like, I don't do it English style or whatever, but I'm a nice guy and like, maybe I could learn if it was really a problem or something.

ELECTRA: What… are you… talking… about?

TOBY: Nothing, forget it, I was just thinking—

BETTINA enters.

BETTINA: Electra, it's time to go. Did you find your make-up case?

ELECTRA: I did.

BETTINA: Go wait in the car, please. I'll be there momentarily.

ELECTRA: Actually, Mom, if you could, like, give me a second—

BETTINA: Go. Now.

ELECTRA: Mom!

BETTINA: Now, Electra.

ELECTRA: Thank God I'm not playing fucking Juliet. (*beat; she turns to TOBY*) 'Bye, Toby.

TOBY: 'Bye.

> *ELECTRA exits. BETTINA waits for her to be out of earshot and then turns to TOBY.*

BETTINA: Mister Kent. I want to make something very clear, so listen closely because I will not be repeating myself: Electra will be turning eighteen in seven months. At that point, due to the ridiculous belief that a person of that age suddenly knows what is best for themselves, I will no longer be able to stop Electra from doing whatever she wants. Until then, however, I intend to make your courtship of her as awkward and difficult as possible. If despite my best efforts you fail to give up and also manage to express your interest in a sincere and gentlemanly fashion at all times, I will refrain from frosting her birthday cake with your bone marrow and perhaps it may work out for you. Assuming we understand each other, you will find that Electra has left her headshot on the table for you. All her vital contact information can be found there. Good luck. Additionally, I would suggest never discussing English style "doing it" with my daughter again. Partly because it's egregiously unseemly to discuss such things with a young lady you barely know, and mostly because it makes you sound like an ignorant ass, pun fully intended. See you at the party.

BETTINA exits. TOBY runs to the table and tears open the envelope ELECTRA left.

TOBY: (*turning around, clutching the head-shot to his chest*) Hey, Anya, would you guys mind if I cut out? I want to run home and change before the party.

ANYA: Not a problem, Toby, see you there.

TOBY: Are you sure? I don't want to leave you stuck with all this—

ANYA: Don't worry about it.

TOBY: Awesome. Thanks. (*he charges towards the door, then stops*) Hey, I just wanted to say, this has been really fucking cool. Like way better than I hoped, you know? You're all really nice people, and I really am glad to have been a part of this!

ANYA: Thank you, Toby. We couldn't have done it without you.

TOBY: Sure you could. I mean, my part was miniscule. I didn't even have any lines till the last scene. And I fucked up half of those on the second night.

ANYA: That's just how second nights go.

TOBY: Right. I know. Now. Which is awesome because now I know that's a thing—because of this show! And that's what I'm saying here. You gave me a chance, when you didn't have to. That's really fucking cool and I really appreciate it.

ANYA: Thank you. (*beat*) Now get out of here, go take a shower—don't just put on cologne—and we will see you at the party.

TOBY: Yeah, see you there! See you there, Gwen!

GWEN: See you.

TOBY exits. WARREN enters.

WARREN: Hey, Anya, where is Lance?

ANYA: He's locking up the theater with Cliff. Everything okay with Bettina?

WARREN: Yup, she's in for the Nurse.

ANYA: I knew she wouldn't turn it down.

WARREN: I'm sure she'll make me wish she had.

He exits. A moment. ANYA smiles at GWEN.

ANYA: You've been awfully quiet. Everything okay?

GWEN: Oh. I always get kind of maudlin at strikes.

ANYA: I'm the same way. I hate it when things end.

GWEN: Me too.

ANYA: But… one thing ending, is another beginning… right?

GWEN: Right. (*looks around*) I think we actually have everything packed away.

ANYA: I think we do too. Help me stack these tubs?

GWEN: Sure. (*they start to stack the tubs neatly against the back wall*) You know, if you want me to come next week, when the costumes all get back from the dry cleaners, I'm happy to do that. I'm sure they're a pain to put away.

ANYA: Not really. I mean, the contemporary ones the actors haven't stolen we'll mostly donate to charity, and the period ones we'll hang in the wardrobe. Should only take a few minutes.

GWEN: Okay, well... still, if you need anything. Let me know. I'd love to stay involved.

ANYA: Great. I'll definitely keep that in mind. There's always plenty to do.

GWEN: I'm sure. I always assumed it would be a lot of work to run a company.

ANYA: At least we have our own theater. Ten years ago, when Lance and I started this, we were renting and it was such a nightmare. Storing things in the garage, carting stuff everywhere. Getting this space was almost more exciting than having kids was. Honestly, I doubt we would have had kids if we hadn't found this place. That was the first time it actually became possible to have a life and a theater company.

GWEN: Well, I've loved working here.

ANYA: We've loved having you.

GWEN: Thanks. That means a lot to me. (*beat*) So, are you in *Romeo and Juliet* too?

ANYA: Yes. Lance and I are Friar Lawrence and Lady Capulet. Respectively.

GWEN: I figured.

ANYA: Well, after Warren's production of *Mother Courage*, I always feel a need to specify. I thought Warren would cast Lance as my husband but he said that would be too cutesy to have us paired up two shows in a row. He's probably right. Lawrence fits Lance better anyway. And Vic will make a good Lord Capulet.

GWEN: Lady Capulet is a good role.

ANYA: Yes. I'm looking forward to doing Shakespeare again. It's been a while for me.

GWEN: I hadn't realized you were going to do *Romeo and Juliet* here.

ANYA: We weren't. *Arcadia* was supposed to be our big cast, big budget show of the season. Warren was supposed to direct *Closer*, but with Josh gone, I'm the only Equity actor in the company and so suddenly, we have more money than usual and the Board felt we could raise some additional funds to cover costumes and a fight choreographer. So why not? It's a show Warren's always wanted to direct and Lance and I figured he could use a little wish fulfillment right now.

GWEN: I think that's very true.

ANYA: How about you? Any plans for what's next?

GWEN: Uh, no. Not really. Auditions I guess.

ANYA: Ah, yes. Auditions. I haven't had to do those in a decade.

GWEN: Must be nice.

ANYA: Yes and no. There's something to be said for knowing you won a part, instead of just being assigned one.

GWEN: I guess. I don't know. For me, the winning has always been pulling off a role, more than getting it in the first place. Getting it always just seems to be luck, of one kind or another. Like sure, maybe you really won the role, but who knows maybe you also just got it because the director's got a crush on you or some passing whim of theirs works in your favor. Your hair is right, or your voice, or whatever. On the other hand, if my performance is good, I know that it's because I made it that way, it's because of what I'm doing and how hard I worked and so if I win that moment of feeling like I truly nailed it, it's so satisfying because I know I earned it, you know? Provided I can, actually, get cast first. Which for some, stupid reason... is the hardest part. (*beat*) Sometimes, I feel like we're all still in middle school gym class together, you know? Vying to be first, praying not to be last, wishing we were more popular, more pretty, more... whatever. Art's supposed to be all about you, your exploration, your expression... but it's really not, is it? It's really about getting through a door someone else has the key to and you have to put all this work, that should be going into your art, into convincing the gate-keeper to just let you in to do it. (*beat*) Since I graduated, I can't count how many times I've wished I'd studied something else. I mean, I could have been a great software engineer, or lawyer or... phlebotomist. Not that I think I would be happy doing anything else, mind you. But then who knows what happy is, right?

WARREN enters.

WARREN: Hey, Anya, Lance said if you're ready to go, he's waiting in the box office. Gwen and I can lock up here.

ANYA: Great. (*to GWEN*) See you at the party?

GWEN: Yes, of course.

ANYA: (*to WARREN*) Don't forget to turn out the lights.

WARREN: Wouldn't dream of running up that electricity bill when I know it would come out of my costume budget.

ANYA: That's absolutely true.

ANYA exits. WARREN looks around the dressing room.

WARREN: This place always freaks me out when it's this clean.

GWEN: Yeah, it's eerie, isn't it? I kind of feel like I'm in the break room at a factory.

WARREN: You kind of are. Only there are no OSHA posters because nobody here has any rights. (*Pause.*) So… Gwen… the young man cuts directly to the chase and offers the young woman the role of Juliet.

GWEN: Oh thank God! I was seriously going to have a break down if you hadn't asked!

WARREN: I'm sorry. I should have sooner but I didn't know I was doing this show until a couple of days ago and then I had to figure out where I was putting company members and… well, honestly, I have no excuse because I knew as soon as I was doing *Romeo and Juliet*, you had to be my Juliet. I assume, by the way, that you are accepting.

GWEN: Of course I'm accepting.

WARREN: Hey, it was not a given. You are a fresh face in this town, but you are a talented woman and you are going to be in demand and out of my reach in no time at all.

GWEN: I'll never be out of your reach.

WARREN: Never is a strong word, don't promise it to anybody, ever. Especially if they aren't asking you to. All I'm asking for is the next three months of your life.

GWEN: Yes. Yes, yes, yes. (*beat*) Who's my Romeo? It's not Toby, is it? Oh, God, please say it's not Toby.

WARREN: It's not Toby. Though Toby is going to play Balthasar. Well, I'm going to offer Toby the chance to play Balthasar. I don't get the impression he's done a lot of Shakespeare and by that I mean any, but I also know he'll work his ass off, so it's a good baby step in. (*beat*) It's not me, either, in case you were worried about that.

GWEN: I didn't think you would cast yourself as Romeo. That never occurred to me.

WARREN: Thank you.

GWEN: Plus you're a little too old for the part.

WARREN: Gee, thanks.

GWEN: I'm just kidding.

WARREN: Eh. You're kind of right. I'm a little past my time to play Romeo. I offered it to Zach, actually, but he is going to be directing at a summer camp for the next few months so he didn't think he could do the rehearsal schedule. He's taking Tybalt instead. Which I think is a better role for him anyway. But that does leave us a gaping hole in a pretty key place.

GWEN: It does. You got a plan?

WARREN: Well, I was thinking of calling Josh and begging him to come back.

GWEN: Really?

WARREN: No. I don't beg anybody for anything. So… we'll be holding auditions. That I'd like you to be at. I want you to pick your Romeo. Subject to my approval, of course and… if you're comfortable doing that.

GWEN: Um… sure. I think that's… kind of fantastic, actually.

WARREN: I thought you'd like it.

GWEN: I do. It'll be nice to be on the other side of the table for a change.

WARREN: Oh no, here we go, already drunk with power.

GWEN: No, no, I will use my influence wisely.

WARREN: Please, use it unwisely. Shake things up around here. We need it. (*A moment. WARREN breathes in deeply, and then exhales.*) Well, here the new life begineth.

GWEN: What?

WARREN: Forster quote. E. M. Forster. You might not know who he is because he never wrote any plays.

GWEN: I know who E.M. Forster is. I read real books too, not just scripts.

WARREN: Well we got that in common. (*beat*) It's what I say whenever I stand in a room I need to expel demons from so that tomorrow I can walk into said room as if I hadn't had my heart broken into a billion pieces there. This room, however, probably needs a full on exorcism. Typical. (*He catches her looking at him.*) What?

GWEN: You know I'm going to have to hug you now, right?

WARREN: One hug. No crying.

GWEN: Deal.

He opens his arms and she walks into them. He fold his arms around her and for a moment they stand in the empty room together. He lets her go.

WARREN: Come on. We have a party to go to, and you're going to drive me.

GWEN: Oh, I figured that. You're going to be fucked up drunk, aren't you?

WARREN: Yup.

> *They reach the door and stop. WARREN turns and takes one last look at the room, GWEN beside him. He reaches out one arm and places his hand on the light switch for the overhead light. He smiles at nothing in particular, then kills the lights.*

End of play.

ACKOWLEDGEMENTS

There are many people who helped make *Pastorella* a thing, from the folks who did the initial staged reading, to those who were part of the first nine-performance production at The EXIT. To all the people involved with that process, listed in the front of this book, I can not thank you enough for coming on this journey with me.

A few additional people need to be thanked for their support and/or advice. These include Kendra Arimoto, Robin Bousel, Lisa Drostova, Alisha Ehrlich, Melissa Fall, Marissa Garcia, Michelle Jasso, Morgan Ludlow, Meghan O'Connor Trowbridge, Amanda Ortmayer, Paul Jennings, Jeunee Simon, Marissa Skudlarek, Robert Sokol, and Nick Trengrove. To anyone I might have forgotten, my apologies, and thank you anyway.

This book wouldn't be possible without the EXIT Press, which wouldn't exist without the efforts of Richard Livingston and Nicole Gluckstern. Carmen White, in specific, was my chief editor on this one, and went through many proofs with a smile.

There are far too many people who inspired *Pastorella* for me to even begin to list them here, plus some of them would probably prefer to remain anonymous. Suffice it to say, each of them is beloved, in my own weird way, for what they brought into the dressing room, and into my life.

ABOUT THE PLAYRIGHT

Stuart Bousel is the Artistic Director of San Francisco indy theater company, No Nude Men Productions, the Executive Producer (and founder) of the San Francisco Olympians Festival (declared by the Guardian to be "Theater Festival Most Likely to Win A Gold Medal" in 2013), the Hospitality Coordinator for the San Francisco Fringe Festival/EXIT Theatre, and the Director of New Work Development for Custom Made Theatre Company. He was the Executive Director (and co-founder) of the San Francisco Theater Pub (winner of the Guardian's "Best of Bay" in 2011), the Publicist for DIVAfest, and served as the chair of the Individual Services Committee for TBA.

He has directed a number of plays for Custom Made, including *M. Butterfly, The Merchant of Venice, Prelude to a Kiss, The Crucible, Grey Gardens, Six Degrees of Separation, The House of Yes*, and *The Lion in Winter*. Other directing credits include *Edward II, Phaedra, Love's Labors Lost, Hamlet*, and *The Desk Set* all with No Nude Men; *Measure For Measure, Dick 3*, and *Taming of the Shrew* with SF Theater Pub; the world premiere of Morgan Ludlow's *Ruth and The Sea* with Wily West Productions; *A Midsummer Night's Dream,*

Twelfth Night, and *The Frogs* for Atmostheatre/Theatre
In the Woods, and *Bag of Dickens* at Killing My Lobster.
He directed the world premieres of Nirmala Nataraj's
The Monk and *The Book of Genesis: Re-mixed and
Remastered*, as well as Susan Sobeloff's *Merchants* and
Allison Luterman's *Oasis*, all for No Nude Men.

As a playwright, his work has been produced
in New York, Dublin, Portland, Tucson, Melbourne,
Seattle, Chicago, and San Francisco. His play *Vincent
of Gilagmesh* was a nominee for the 2001 MAC Award;
his play *Matthew 33:6* was a finalist for the Sky Cooper
Award in 2007; and his play *Wild Blue Peaks* was a
finalist at HUMANA in 2002. He co-wrote the John C.
Cosgrove Award winning short film *Insomnia* in 2000,
and his play *Everybody Here Says Hello!* (produced by
Wily West Productions) received the Theatre Bay Area
Award for Outstanding World Premiere in 2014, and
was nominated for Best Original Script by the Bay Area
Theatre Critics Circle in 2015.

He has three times had work featured in the
Bay One Acts Festival: *Housebroken* in 2010, *Speak
Roughly* in 2011, and *Brainkill* in 2012. He adapted
the novel *Giant Bones*, by Peter S. Beagle, in 2010,
and the memoir *Rat Girl*, by Kristin Hersh, in 2014
(also nominated for Outstanding World Premiere,
TBA Awards). His play *Pastorella* was nominated for
the 2015 Theatre Bay Area Award for Outstanding
World Premiere. Additional works, *Adventures in Tech
(With Pillow Talk On The Side)* and *Twins,* received
premiere productions at PianoFight, and *Gone Dark*
at Otherworld Theatre Company. He has also written
several children's plays, including *Polyxena in Orbit,
The Elephant in the Room*, and *Jason Lives: The Story or
the Argo-nots!*

He is the recipient of the SF Weekly's "Ringmaster Award" in Best of the Bay 2013. Other works include penning the online short film *Wish U Were Here* for Hosteling International, the novel *Dry Country*, the libretto of the short opera *Devil's Deal* for Opera Theatre Unlimited, and co-editing two collections of new work by Bay Area playwrights, *Songs of Hestia* (2012), and *Heavenly Bodies* (2014), both published by EXIT Press. Each include a full-length play by him: *Juno En Victoria* and *Hyperion To A Satyr*, respectively.

With Megan Cohen he co-founded the monthly Bay Area writer/actor meet up Saturday Write Fever.

His Bay Area acting credits including the Actor's Theatre of San Francisco (*Jacob Marley's Christmas Carol*), The EXIT Theatre (*Confessions of a Catholic Child*), The Bay One Acts Festival (*Future of the Female*) and The Custom Made Theatre Company (*Chess*).

More information about his work can be found at www.stuartbousel.com.

MORE PLAYS FROM EXIT PRESS

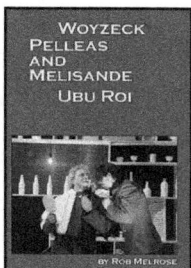

Woyzeck, Pelleas and Melisande, Ubu Roi: translated by Rob Melrose

"Rob Melrose is a kind of magician, and his theater, Cutting Ball, is one of the most exciting and integrity-filled enterprises going in the sometimes-shabby field of the American theater. These translations, lucid and sharp, are a beautiful testimony to the value of Rob's achievement." — Oskar Eustis

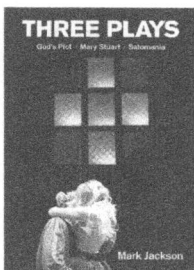

Three Plays by Mark Jackson

Playwright/director Mark Jackson has made his name as a first-class theatrical provocateur. Gutsy showmanship, brainy literary instincts and laser-sharp satire mark his canon."—San Jose Mercury News. The second collection of plays by Mark Jackson includes three plays based on incredible historic events: *God's Plot*, *Mary Stuart*, and *Salomania*.

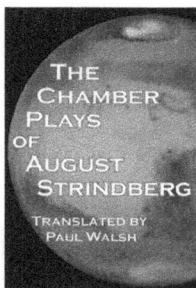

The Chamber Plays of August Strindberg: Translated by Paul Walsh

New translations by Yale drama professor Paul Walsh of the intimate chamber plays of August Strindberg, one of the major pioneers of naturalism in the theater: *The Ghost Sonata*, *Storm*, *Burned House*, *The Pelican*, and *The Black Glove*.

EXIT Press is the publishing division of EXIT Theatre, a San Francisco theater company founded in 1983. www.exitpress.org

www.ingramcontent.com/pod-product-compliance
Lightning Source LLC
Chambersburg PA
CBHW060401050426
42449CB00009B/1842